Your birthday is so important to me,
I could fill a book with my feelings.

To:

From:

Date:

THE
Too-Bad-It's-Your-Birthday
BOOK

Tender Sentiments to Make Your Wrinkly Face
Break into a Toothless Grin

JAMES DALE

STARK BOOKS

Andrews McMeel
Publishing

Kansas City

01 02 03 04 05 RDS 10 9 8 7 6 5 4 3 2 1

ISBN: 0-7407-1112-1

Library of Congress Catalog Card Number 00-108491

Book design by Holly Camerlinck

THE
Too-Bad-It's-Your-Birthday
BOOK

So you're having another birthday.

That's a tragic pity
with no redeeming aspects.

Life is like a bowl of cereal.

And these are the soggy years.

A Birthday Fantasy:

A sexy European fashion model who speaks no English
waits on you hand and foot.

Hey, I warned you it was a fantasy.

You know, nothing in the world
is more important to me than your birthday . . .

. . . unless my cell phone rings.

If you're like me, you're attracted to smart women . . .

. . . who are naked.

Birthday boy,
we grew up together.

Well, one of us grew up.

Who's older . . .

. . . you or the Earth?

Remember when we were kids
and we hunted for fossils?

And now we're what we hunted for.

Birthday boy,
you're so mature.

You must be *way* older than me.

Don't get down about getting older.

Some wart-covered lizards live to be over two hundred.
(But nobody wants to touch them.)

Some people say
if you can get a princess to kiss you on your birthday
you turn from a frog into a prince.

Looks like it didn't work.

You aren't the type to make a birthday wish for one of those cheap, easy women.

Unless it's just for the day.

So, it's your birthday.
Things could be worse.

It could be your birthday
and you could clean public urinals for a living.

Guys have all the fun,
swearing, smoking, gambling, and drinking.

But women pretty much run the world.

Now that you're older,
you can admit it.

You watch the Weather Channel.

On your birthday,
someone who cares about you will make dinner . . .

. . . reservations.

Birthday Test:

- Does it seem like newspapers and books are printed in smaller type each year?
- Do you believe the freedom to complain about creaky joints should be in the Bill of Rights?
- Are you in favor of a tax on people who are younger than you?

Happy birthday to a guy who appreciates the symphony, ballet, and opera . . .

. . . as great places to nap.

You know what's great about celebrating your birthday by watching TV?

You don't have to go anywhere.

I don't want to sound like an old curmudgeon but . . .

Why do people pierce their tongues?

Hey, even at our age, we're still swingers.

But now when we swing,
we get dizzy and have to go to bed by 11 P. M.

W as it Patrick Henry who said on his birthday:

"Give me something expensive or give me nothing at all"?

I could sit and stare at the wall all day contemplating your birthday.

If . . . the wall had a big-screen TV on it.

Remember when you were a kid
and you stayed in the bathtub and got all wrinkly?

Guess you stayed too long?

Honest . . . *ha-ha* . . . *hee-hee* . . .

You still look young and virile . . . *HA-HA-HA!*

Scientists now have a theory on
why you feel bad on your birthday.

You're very old.

Your friends got together to light
all your birthday candles.

Oops, not enough friends.

It was Neanderthal man who first gathered his fellow cavemen together after a hunt, drank an early form of brewed ale, and . . .

. . . had farting contests.

An International Birthday Message:

As ze French say, you're *très* old.

If you lie on your back and stare at the ceiling,
pretty soon the whole room seems like it's upside down.

(When we get older, it doesn't take much to entertain us.)

Condolences on your birthday.

I'm sorry to hear your youth has passed away.

A Birthday Thought
That's Not Politically Correct:

Don't you miss the good old days before recycling
when you could just throw stuff away?

A Birthday Thought
That's Not Politically Correct:

What's so wrong with calling a good-looking chick
a "babe"?

A Birthday Thought
That's Not Politically Correct:

Do we really want to have compost heaps?

A Birthday Thought
That's Not Politically Correct:

Why be shallow and marry just for looks
when you can marry for something meaningful, like money?

I have your actual age written on a piece of paper . . .

. . . so don't piss me off.

It's now estimated the universe is a trillion years old.

That's two years older than you.

On your birthday,
I'm not going to make anymore insulting comments
about your age.

It wouldn't be nice to a decrepit, senile geezer like you.

Sometimes your hearing goes as you get older.

SOMETIMES IT'S YOUR EYES.

On your birthday,
every minute I spend without you is agony . . .

. . . except Thursday nights
when there's really good stuff on TV.

<big>C</big>elebrate with this
special birthday blend coffee . . .

. . . extra caffeine and a dash of Viagra.

Life is a roller coaster.
Exciting on the way up . . .

. . . then suddenly you want to throw up!

I put a little piece of string on this ball
every time you had a birthday.

Now I have this huge stupid ball of string.

Hey, have you heard the one about . . .

Forget it—at your age you've heard 'em all.

Remember 3-D?

If you do, you're even older than me.

Before you celebrate your birthday,
make sure your girlfriend or wife has one of these.

They make even tiny things look huge.

Here's a Fun Birthday Game:

1. Write down your age   _____
2. Subtract 10   <u> -10 </u>
3. Imagine that's your age   _____

Okay, game's over, add the 10 back.

Me and the boys would like you to have a happy birthday . . .

. . . or else.

Birthdays are like professional hockey.

A lot of fun for a while, but sooner or later
you lose your teeth.

I was going to sing "Happy Birthday"
to you in Flemish.

But I was afraid I'd get Flem on your cake.

I got you a special birthday present.

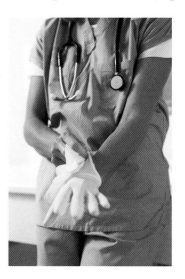

Now, let's see if we can find it.

In honor of your birthday

I have gas.

You've had so many birthdays, it finally happened:

There's nobody older than you.

Birthday boy,
you have an air about you.

But a hot shower and a change of clothes should take care of it.

Look, up in the sky.
A flock of pigeons is spelling out
HAPPY BIRTHDAY.

Watch out! They had lunch at a taco stand.

I know a dog is supposed to be your best friend . . .

. . . but I won't poop in your living room.

I wouldn't tell anyone your real age
for all the money in the world.

But for a cold brew on a hot day,
I'd spill everything.

It's your birthday.

Okay, enough about you, mine's next.